Where Are You Going?

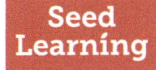

school

park

library

playground

supermarket

mall

home

movie theater

Where are you going?

I'm going to school.

Where are you going?

I'm going to the park.

Where are you going?

I'm going to the library.

Where are you going?

I'm going to the supermarket.

Where are you going?

I'm going to the playground.

Where are you going?

I'm going home!

Let's learn more about Germany.

Currywurst